The Lost Art of Silence
Awakening to Wonder
Alex Ngeno

Quiet Harbour Press

Copyright © 2026

All rights reserved.

No part of this publication may be reproduced, stored in a retrieval system, or transmitted in any form or by any means, electronic, mechanical, photocopying, recording, or otherwise, without the prior written permission of the copyright owner, except for brief quotations used in reviews or scholarly work.

Notes on the Artwork

The images in this book are part of the journey.

The images in this edition have been prepared for black-and-white print to suit library and archival circulation. Where colour carried essential symbolic meaning, images have been thoughtfully reworked for monochrome so that their intent remains clear through contrast, texture, and form.

They were created through a blend of digital illustration and AI-assisted creative tools as instruments for shaping the symbolic language that runs alongside these essays. Many of the themes explored here, silence, longing, identity, ancestry, and transcendence, resist literal depiction. When guided with care and intention, these tools allow metaphor to take visual form, giving shape to what is often unseen.

The visual works accompanying the essays are not illustrations in the traditional sense. They function as symbolic visual meditations, designed to echo the metaphysical, existential, and spiritual questions explored in the text rather than to explain or depict them.

All visual works were conceived, directed, and curated by the author as integral components of the book's contemplative structure.

Each image is intended to be encountered slowly, in the same contemplative spirit as the writing. They are placed at the threshold of each essay, offering a pause: a quiet doorway between the reader's daily life and the interior landscape the chapter invites them to enter.

All images are original works created specifically for this book and are used with full commercial rights.

These artworks are not decorative. They are invitations.

If the essays are meditations, the images are the breath before them.

To engage with the artwork:

- **Pause before reading.**

Let the image settle. Notice its mood, its texture, its silence.

- **Observe what it stirs.**

A memory, a question, a feeling which are all part of the conversation.

- **Let the symbols work quietly.**

Not every meaning needs to be named; some are meant to accompany you rather than explain themselves.

The artwork and the writing are two halves of a single gesture both reaching toward what cannot be spoken directly. Together, they create a visual and contemplative path through *The Lost Art of Silence* trilogy.

These books are not only meant to be read but to be experienced.

Breath.

Acknowledgement

With gratitude to those who kept faith with the quiet: my family, friends, and early readers who saw this book not just as words, but as prayer. The teachers in the League of Gentlemen, who told me not to die with a book in me. To the students who inspired many of these reflections, and to the readers who continue the conversation.

Dedication

For my father, fondly known as 'fathe', who bought me my first literary magazines and helped build my imagination, and whose quiet strength taught me that silence is its own kind of eloquence.

Contents

Prologue	1
1. The Man of Clocks	4
2. Nature's Naked Truth	7
3. The River Teaches Us	10
4. Ash an Ember	13
5. Silence	16
6. The Day the Island Breathes	19
7. The Silence Between Us	23
8. The Courage of Stillness	26
9. Reflections in Bali	29
10. Where The Wind Prays	33
11. Sacred in the Small	36
12. The Ceremony of Small Things	40
13. The Silence of God	43
14. Reflections at Vivonne Bay	46
15. The Goldilocks Planet	49
16. The Blue Dot	52
17. The Hole in the Heart	54

18. The Quiet Between Two Homelands	57
19. Letter to the Boy I Was	60
20. The Machine Hearts	65
21. After the Noise	69
22. When the World Forgets to Listen	72
23. Becoming the Ocean	75
24. The Song of the Seeker	78
25. The Blood of the Earth	81
26. Make Way for Man	84
27. When Listening Becomes Longing	87
28. Author's Note	91
29. Epilogue	94
About the author	96

Prologue

Before every beginning, there is a hush.

The world waits, as it did before light first trembled across the waters, before the first cry named the first dawn. That same hush lingers still, hidden beneath the engines of our busy days. It hums beneath the noise of traffic and speech, beneath our endless need to explain. And if we listen carefully, we can hear it: the soundless pulse from which everything rises, the heartbeat of the unspoken.

We live in an age of perpetual declaration: every thought broadcast, every silence filled. Yet some truths cannot be told, only tended. The ancients knew this. They built temples where echo and emptiness were integral to the design, where prayer was not merely words but also posture, breath, and presence. They understood that silence is not absence but origin. It is where the soul learns its first vocabulary: waiting, wonder, awe.

This book is a map through that inner landscape. It does not promise answers, only clarity. It follows the pilgrim through three movements of stillness: the Long Silence of listening, the Offerings of illumination, and the Return to grace. Each part is both a descent and an ascent, a turning of the same circle. You will not find doctrine here, only the quiet companionship of reflection. A reminder that every voice needs an echo, and every echo begins in silence.

To read these pages is not to escape the world but to meet it differently, to walk slower, to see deeper, to breathe as if each inhale were prayer. For silence is not the opposite of sound; it is the soil from which sound draws its meaning. Without it, the world becomes a blur of unanchored noise. With it, everything holds its proper weight: the call of a bird, the strike of a match, the whisper of someone you love saying nothing at all.

In every life, there comes a moment when words can no longer hold what the heart knows. That is where this journey begins. The pilgrim stands at the edge of speech, empty-handed, listening. Behind him, the world of explanations; ahead, the vast uncharted realm of being. He steps forward, not to conquer, but to remember.

The art of silence is the art of returning to breath, to body, to belonging. It teaches us that to be still is not to withdraw, but to awaken. And somewhere in that stillness, the ordinary becomes luminous: the curve of a leaf, the warmth of sunlight through a window, the steady rhythm of a sleeping heart. All of it prayer. All of it praise.

So, before you turn the page, pause. Listen.

Let the noise settle. Let the hush speak.

For everything worth hearing begins here.

The Man of Clocks

The clocks of our lives do not tick outward but inward.

At the edge of a courtyard, beneath a quiet sun, stands a sculpture of a man on a bicycle. His entire body is covered in miniature clocks, each one frozen at a different hour. Time has gathered upon him like dust, like memory. It has taken shape and weight and become almost human.

He sits upright, calm, his gaze fixed on an invisible horizon. Behind him trail bronze vessels, tear-shaped and glimmering, bound to his bicycle by thin chains. They tug gently, as if heavy with what they hold. Watching him, I feel a strange paradox: a man built from time itself, yet bound to stillness, forever poised between motion and rest.

He reminds me of us. We live layered with the sediment of our own hours, shaped not by how much time we *use* but by how much time has *used* us. The clocks upon his body do not mark the passing of days; they mark the making of a soul. Each small dial holds an experience. Each frozen moment is a memory turned to metal.

Dalí once painted clocks melting into the landscape, symbols of decay and impermanence. Here, the clocks have hardened. They no longer droop or flee the body. They cling to it. Time, in this sculpture, is not dissolving but accumulating. Yet both visions tell the same truth: time cannot be conquered. Whether it melts or hardens, whether it slips away or weighs us down, it outlasts the body that carries it.

And still, there is peace in this figure. Though he is made entirely of clocks, he does not strain beneath them. He seems reconciled with their burden, as though he has made a quiet covenant with time. Perhaps that is what it means to grow older: to carry our hours openly, to accept both rust and shine, to let the years mark us without shame.

As I turn to leave, the light shifts. The bronze figure glows faintly gold. For a moment, the clocks shimmer as though alive, not ticking in unison, but in a soft, imagined harmony, each marking a breath within a breath. Time continues, as it must. Yet in that small moment, it feels as if it pauses, not stopping but simply breathing.

We, too, move through time like riders on an unseen bicycle, our bodies veined with the moments that shaped us. We travel through seasons, sometimes swiftly, sometimes wearily, but always onward. The miracle is not that we reach the horizon, but that we continue despite the weight we carry. Each breath is a quiet tick; each heartbeat a reminder that even as time melts, something within us endures.

The man of clocks is not a warning. He is a benediction: a reminder that our meaning is not found in outrunning time, but in accepting its companionship.

Nature's Naked Truth

Nature does not hurry, because it already belongs to itself.

There are mornings when the earth seems to stir before us. The air trembles with a kind of listening, and the light is so pure it feels awake. In such moments, the world strips itself of all ornaments, no noise, no spectacle, just presence. That is nature's naked truth: it exists not to impress but to remind.

To stand before a mountain, or a field washed by rain, or a leaf trembling in a pool of sunlight, is to realise how little we comprehend endurance. Nature does not hurry, yet everything in it transforms. The seed breaks open in the dark; the river carves through stone; the bird trusts the wind without question. It is we who have forgotten how to belong to time.

We chase permanence, in buildings, in fame, in data stored on invisible clouds, yet nature shows us that all genuine beauty depends on change. The flower that never fades is not immortal; it is artificial. The tree grows by shedding. Even decay, seen rightly, is a kind of prayer, a return of form to source, of life to the soil that formed it.

Once, walking after rain, I saw the earth steaming like a body exhaling. Each droplet clung to a blade of grass like a tiny lens, refracting whole worlds within. I thought of how little we notice such wonders. We speak of nature as if it were scenery, but it is scripture, written in sunlight and shadow, revised daily, endlessly renewed.

If the earlier centuries taught man to dominate nature, perhaps our era must learn to listen again. To listen not as tourists or consumers, but as participants. The forest does not speak in words, yet it converses with us, in the whisper of leaves, the rhythm of waves, the slow choreography of clouds. These are sentences of patience. To read them is to remember that time is not our enemy but our companion.

There is an honesty in the wilderness that terrifies and heals. Nature does not flatter us. It reflects what we are, fleeting, vulnerable, yet luminous in our awareness. The wind erases our footprints as easily as it shapes dunes. The waves that destroy also polish stone to brilliance.

There is no cruelty in this, only completion. To love nature is to accept that loss is part of the design.

Perhaps redemption is nothing more than remembering this kinship, that we are not masters of the earth, but part of its memory. The soil that stains our shoes once held stars. The water we drink has passed through clouds and veins alike. Everything belongs to everything.

When the evening comes and the first stars appear, I sometimes imagine that the world exhales, relieved that, for a few hours, it can simply exist. The insects hum, the wind folds itself into sleep, and the dark returns the sky to itself. In that stillness, something eternal stirs, not outside us, but within. Nature's naked truth is that we, too, are nature. Our minds are forests of thought, our veins rivers of time. To care for the earth is to care for the part of it that breathes through us.

The River Teaches Us

Every river knows the way home, even when we do not.

My favourite writer once spoke of a river that was hesitant to enter the ocean. It trembled at the thought of losing itself, of being swallowed by something vast and unknowable. But when it finally reached the sea, the river discovered it had not vanished. It had become something greater than it could ever imagine.

That story has followed me all my life. For time itself is a river, and so are we. We begin in the highlands of birth, pure and narrow and swift, cutting paths through rock and memory. Along the way, we gather silt, stories, and scars. We erode, we deepen, we change course. Yet always there is the pull of something larger, the ocean of belonging that draws us onward.

I have stood beside many rivers. The Naibor of my childhood, pale and restless. The Ganges, heavy with ashes and prayer. The Murray, whose red banks whisper of age and drought. Each one taught me something about patience, about letting go, about how water carries both memory and forgiveness.

In Africa, rivers are more than water; they are spirit. They breathe life into the land. Without them, crops wither, cattle die, and the rhythm of life breaks. Many ceremonies, especially rites of passage, are performed by the riverside in the quiet of early dawn. The cold water touches the skin, and the elders speak words that awaken both body and spirit. There, by the flowing water, we remember that we come from the same source, that purity, courage, and renewal are not found in temples but in the rhythm of living water.

A river never rushes the mountain. It knows the mountain will yield in time. It does not hoard the past; it keeps moving, trusting the bends, the rocks, the rain. Even when it floods, even when it runs dry, it remains faithful to its purpose, to reach the sea.

Perhaps this is what life keeps teaching us, quietly and continuously: to trust the current even when the way is rough. To understand that surrender is not defeat; it is the recognition that we were never meant to remain still.

When I watch a river, I see the story of the soul. We begin as something small and separate, fearing the vastness ahead. But the ocean, that immense silence where all waters meet, is not our end. It is our homecoming.

Maybe that is what the river knows, what it tries to teach us with every shimmer and turn, that only by losing ourselves do we truly discover what we are.

Ash an Ember

We mourn loudly so the light can find us again.

Among my people, the Kalenjin, the dead are laid to rest with their heads facing east, toward Asis, the rising sun. It is not merely tradition but belief that the departed should look toward renewal, toward the light that returns even after the longest night.

In my homeland, when a great statesman passes on, the Luo tribe will gather in ritual and song. The air carries the sound of *Tero Buru*, the mourning procession where men run, shout, and strike their shields to drive away the spirit of death. It is grief, yes, but also defiance, a declaration that life, though wounded, continues. Every culture has this ritualistic fight with Death.

I have seen this same sacred defiance in other corners of the world.

On the banks of the Ganges, I once watched burning bodies drift upon the holy river, the flames flickering like tongues of prayer. There was no fear, only release.

In Mexico, during the Festival of the Dead, skulls are painted with laughter, and candles burn through the night. The living dine with the dead because love refuses to end.

Among Aboriginal elders, I once heard songlines sung to guide the departed back to the Dreaming. Their voices moved with the wind, carrying echoes of the first songs of creation.

Every culture, it seems, knows what the heart has always known, that we are dust, but the dust remembers.

During Lent, Catholics kneel as a priest marks their foreheads with ashes and whispers, "From dust you came, and to dust you shall return." It is a humbling truth, but not a hopeless one. The ash is not only a symbol of ending; it is the beginning of renewal. What burns becomes light. What dies returns to the soil and feeds new life.

Rituals, in all their languages, are our conversation with eternity.

We bury, we sing, we light fires, not because we understand death, but because we cannot bear to let meaning die with the body.

They say every atom in us was once forged in the heart of a dying star. The iron in our blood, the calcium in our bones, the carbon that shapes our skin, all were born from explosions older than language.

So, when we speak of 'ashes to ashes, dust to dust', we are not speaking of endings, but of returning. The dust is not earth alone; it is the memory of light.

Long before we built temples, before we whispered prayers or carved gods from stone, the universe was already praying, burning, collapsing, scattering itself so that one day we might breathe and wonder.

Perhaps that is why fire has always been sacred.

The cremation flame, the candle on an altar, the hearth in a dark hut, each reminds us of our shared origin. We kneel before fire because, in some deep way, it recognises us.

We are stardust remembering itself, light that has learned to ask questions.

And maybe, when we die, the stars are simply calling us home.

Silence

Silence is not the absence of sound, but the presence of self- Rumi

Once, silence was a teacher. It spoke through the hush before dawn, through the pause between words, through the long breath taken before answering a difficult question. It shaped thought, nurtured patience, and gave meaning to what was said. Today, silence feels almost forbidden, an interruption in a world that cannot stop talking.

Everywhere, sound surrounds us. Screens hum, messages ping, voices pour endlessly into the air. We fill every gap and every pause, as if stillness itself were dangerous. In classrooms, homes, streets, and even places of worship, the noise is constant, not the noise of life, but of avoidance. It drowns out the things we fear to face: our doubts, our longing, our very selves.

I remember sitting in a room full of students when a storm cut the power. For a few seconds, everything went dark and utterly quiet. No keyboards clicking, no notifications, no laughter, only breathing. Some students shifted nervously, and others smiled in embarrassment. The silence lasted barely ten seconds, but it felt eternal. When the lights returned, relief rippled through the room. I realised then how unfamiliar silence had become; how uneasy we are in our own company.

Silence is not emptiness. It is space, the air in which thought expands. The mind, like a flame, needs oxygen, not the gusts of constant attention but the calm that allows it to breathe. Without silence, we become brittle and reactive. We confuse noise with meaning, motion with purpose.

The ancients knew silence as a virtue. Pythagoras required his students to keep silent for years before speaking about philosophy. The desert monks withdrew into wordless prayer to hear the whisper of God. Even now, a simple pause before speech can carry wisdom: the awareness that words matter, that thought must precede sound.

In losing silence, we have lost more than quiet; we have lost depth. We skim the surface of experience like stones skipping across water, never staying long enough to see what lies beneath. Even in conversation, we speak to answer, not to understand. The pause, the small, sacred space between one person's thought and another's, has collapsed. We listen not to be changed, but to confirm what we already believe.

Sometimes I think silence is the actual language of the soul. Every faith and every philosophy points toward it in some form. The mystics call it contemplation. The poets call it wonder. The scientists call it awe. It is the space where awareness turns inward, where we stop performing and begin to perceive.

To be silent is to remember that being, not doing, is our most honest act.

The Day the Island Breathes

In silence, even the stars return to their original brightness.

On the day of Nyepi, the Balinese silence the island. No engines. No screens. No scrolling feeds.

For one whole day, the world exhales, and what has long been stifled by noise finally breathes freely again.

Time loosens its grip. The roads lie empty, the beaches fall still, and even the wind seems to move more gently, as if afraid to disturb the spell. From the mountains to the sea, Bali inhales, and then, for twenty-four hours, holds its collective breath.

They call it the Day of Silence.

Planes are grounded. Shops close their doors. Fishermen stay home. Families gather in candlelight, their homes dimmed, their hearts attentive. The island disappears into shadow, not as a gesture of absence, but of reverence.

They say that on this night the spirits wander, crossing from the unseen into the seen. And so the people remain indoors, letting the island itself pray. The air feels older somehow, thick with a wisdom that existed before the first motor turned, before electricity pulsed through the veins of the world.

In that silence, you can hear the earth remembering itself.

The sea sighs with a slow rhythm. The stars burn with original fire. Somewhere in the distance, a temple bell trembles once, then lets its sound dissolve into the dark.

It is not an empty quiet. It is a living one, the kind that listens deeply.

Nyepi is a day of cleansing, a ritual of shared humility. An entire island chooses to step aside, to stop imposing its will upon the world. In that shared stillness, humanity and nature breathe together again, like two halves of a long-forgotten prayer.

I remember walking through Seminyak on the evening before Nyepi. The air was heavy with incense, and the sound of drums echoed through the alleys as people carried their *ogoh-ogoh*, giant paper demons with glaring eyes and wild hair, through the streets. They were paraded, confronted, and burned, as if to purge the year's accumulated noise. When the flames died, the drums stopped. A sudden, sacred hush fell across the island, as though even the gods had turned inward.

The next morning, nothing. No cars, no radios, no engines. The loudest sound was a bird's wings slicing through the dawn. I had never heard silence so complete. It was not an absence. It was presence. It felt as if the island itself were meditating.

Perhaps this is what we all crave, though we rarely admit it: a day without the world's endless commentary. A day to hear what the heart speaks when nothing interrupts.

Nyepi teaches that silence is not withdrawal. It is participation of another kind, the sound of creation recalibrating. It reminds us that we do not need to fill every hour to justify being alive. The Western world fears quiet; it confuses movement with meaning. But here, stillness is strength. To stop is to honour the rhythm of the universe, to recognise that existence itself is sacred enough.

As night deepens, the sky seems to widen. Without light, the stars multiply. Without distraction, the soul recalls its original proportions. For one day, humanity steps back and creation continues without us, unburdened, perfect, whole.

And in that revelation lies both humility and peace: the knowing that the world will go on, even when we remain silent.

Maybe we need our own Nyepi, wherever we are. A day without engines, without screens, without performance. A day when the only task is to listen to the breathing of the trees, the rhythm of the heart, the ancient murmur of the sea.

When the day ends, the island slowly wakes. Lamps are lit again, the first motorcycles hum, and the waves reclaim their restless voice. Yet something lingers: a faint vibration of balance restored, the memory of how stillness feels when it belongs to everyone.

For those few hours, the earth was whole once more.

May we all find our own Nyepi, after every storm, every feast, every frantic holiday of our restless age.

May we remember how to fall quiet long enough to hear the universe whisper what it has been saying since the beginning: that silence is not the absence of life, but its presence.

The Silence Between Us

Between words, something is still being said.

There is a silence that grows between people, not suddenly but slowly, almost unnoticed. It gathers in the pauses we avoid, in the truths we delay, in the thoughts we decide are safer kept inside. We imagine silence to be empty, yet in relationships it is often the fullest space of all. It carries the disappointments we never voice, the apologies we do not know how to offer, the hopes we fear will sound foolish if spoken aloud.

Many relationships do not end in anger; they end in silence. A couple stops explaining themselves. Friends drift because neither wants to admit they feel neglected. Families lose connection not through conflict but through the habit of withholding. Most misunderstandings begin long before any argument. They begin with a silence that hardens into assumption, then into suspicion, then into a narrative neither person ever intended.

But quietness is not always destructive. At its best, it creates the conditions for honesty. Some of the most important truths emerge only after the noise has fallen away, for example, when two people sit long enough with their discomfort to finally say what matters. Silence can clear a space for compassion. It can soften defensiveness. It can remind us that listening is not inferior to speaking; it is often the more courageous act.

To love someone well is to learn their silences. The quiet of exhaustion is different from the quiet of hurt. The quiet of reflection is not the quiet of resentment. We do not need fluency in psychology to understand this; we need attention. Simple, steady attention to the human being in front of us. Most people are not waiting for perfect words. They are waiting for presence.

Perhaps strength in relationships is not measured in how easily two people talk, but in how gently they can be quiet together. Silence does not have to be a threat. It can be a kind of trust-the shared confidence that not every feeling needs to be translated into speech for it to be understood.

In the end, the silence between us reveals the truth of our bonds. When it becomes a barrier, it warns us that repair is needed. When it becomes a refuge, it shows that we have created something safe. What matters is not the existence of silence, but the meaning we allow it to hold.

The Courage of Stillness

Stillness is the courage to face what noise keeps us from seeing.

There is a kind of courage in quiet. It asks us to face what we usually drown out: our fears, our sorrow, our unmet hopes. It strips away the chatter of the mind and leaves us standing before what is real. And in that exposure, there is calm. Silence does not judge or demand; it simply holds. Like the pause before a wave breaks, it carries everything that might yet come.

We do not need to leave the world to find it. Silence can live within sound if we learn to listen differently: in the hush beneath rain, in the breath between heartbeats, in the gentleness of waiting before we speak. The art lies in noticing. With practice, silence stops feeling like an absence and becomes a presence, a companion that steadies rather than isolates.

If I have learned anything from the quiet moments that remain, the corridors before dawn, the first light after rain, it is that silence restores balance. It reminds us that not everything needs an answer and that wisdom grows in the pauses. Like the spaces between musical notes, silence gives shape to the melody of life.

Perhaps this is what redemption means in our noisy age: a return to listening. To hear again the voice beneath all voices, the one that says: *Be still, and know.*

Be Still.

Be.

In that stillness, we are not diminished but made whole. Silence, far from empty, is full of presence, of promise, of peace.

Reflections in Bali

In silence, even the stars return to their original brightness.

Each morning, before the first horns sound and the engines wake, a woman steps out onto her veranda. She carries a small woven basket made of palm leaf. Inside there are flowers, a few grains of rice, a sliver of banana and a drop of perfume. She bends, places it on the ground, lights a stick of incense and folds her hands in prayer. Smoke curls upward, delicate and fragrant, carrying her devotion into the unseen.

There is a profound simplicity in this act: an offering not meant to be seen, not even to be heard, but to be felt. Across the island, doorways and pavements bloom with these tiny gifts to the gods. Each one is fleeting, gone by nightfall, yet renewed at dawn. In these gestures, faith becomes rhythm, not doctrine but daily pulse.

Watching this ritual unfold, I often think about the nature of devotion. The modern world prizes display: faith too often becomes performance. But these offerings are quiet, almost hidden, made to be stepped over by the unseeing and washed away by rain.

There is another rhythm that defines this place, the constant hum of movement. Everywhere, motorbikes weave like shoals of fish, carrying whole families, crates of fruit, baskets of flowers, children holding tight to their parents. The island never truly stops moving, and yet within that motion there is reverence.

It makes me wonder whether our own search for meaning has become too still, too self-conscious. The people here seem to have found harmony between action and prayer, between the rush of living and the pause of offering.

I remember walking down a narrow lane at dusk. The light was gold, almost liquid. From somewhere came the shimmering rhythm of gamelan, those metallic tones that ripple like water. Children laughed. A man swept fallen petals into a small pile. Dogs slept beside scooters. Everything felt precise yet unarranged, ordinary yet illuminated. It was as though the island itself was breathing a blessing.

In that moment, I understood something about faith that no sermon could teach. It is not about the distance between earth and heaven, but the dialogue between them. The offering is not a transaction; it is a declaration, a way of saying, *I am here, and I remember You.* It is humanity's oldest conversation, spoken through hands and smoke and colour.

There is also an honesty to impermanence here. The offerings rot, the flowers wilt, the incense burns out. No one mourns their passing. Tomorrow, they will begin again. It is a lesson the modern spirit resists, that the value of a thing is not in its endurance but in its giving. To create something beautiful and let it vanish may be the purest form of faith.

And what of the demons, the fierce statues with bulging eyes and sharp teeth that guard every gate? They too are part of the dialogue. They remind us that good and evil, beauty and fear, coexist within us. The same hands that scatter petals also carve monsters. Yet in that duality lies truth. Holiness means little if it denies its shadow. The balance of both is what makes the world whole.

As night falls, the last trails of incense drift upward like thin prayers. I find myself breathing slower, more aware. The day's noise softens into the quiet murmur of waves. In the distance, a temple bell sounds, low, resonant, enduring. Its echo moves through the darkened streets, touching even those who do not believe.

The next morning, I see the same woman stepping out again with her basket of flowers. The air is cool, the sky pale with new light. She bends, places her offering on the ground and the smoke rises once more, a quiet dialogue renewed. I watch, and in that simple gesture, I see the reflection of all humanity: the longing to reach beyond ourselves, to offer something back to the mystery that sustains us.

Night comes softly in Bali. The last colours fade from the horizon, and the wind that once lifted the kites drifts downward to rest. In the hush that follows, the world feels suspended, as if the sky itself were holding its breath. What rises must one day return: the flame to ash, the prayer to silence, the spirit to its source.

I thought about how every element has its moment of surrender, air giving way to fire, fire to dust, dust to memory. What we release does not disappear; it alters its form.

Perhaps that is the quiet covenant of existence, that nothing is ever truly lost, only transformed.

As the first stars appeared above the still fields, I began to understand what the ancients meant by renewal. The flight of the kite, the glow of the ember, the whisper of prayer, all belong to the same conversation.

Where The Wind Prays

Some prayers do not rise on words, but on wind.

In Bali, even the sky feels inhabited. Everywhere you look, kites rise, hundreds of them, straining unseen threads, fluttering like bright fragments of prayer against the blue.

On some afternoons, you can stand by the rice terraces and see entire families gathered in the fields, faces tilted upward, holding their lines like lifelines. The kites twist and hum in the wind, not toys but instruments of faith. Each one is a conversation with the heavens; a question carried beyond reach.

It is said that when the wind lifts a kite, the spirits take notice. The sky, once indifferent, listens. For a moment, earth and air speak the same language.

I once watched a boy run barefoot through a field, his laughter chasing the tail of a red kite as it climbed higher and higher. His father stood nearby, hands behind his back, watching. He did not step in, only smiled, as if he knew the lesson would teach itself: to fly something is to let it go, and to let it go is to learn trust.

I thought then of the old US Air Force anthem, "Off we go into the wild blue yonder, climbing high into the sun." It was a song of ascent, of men who believed they could outclimb fate. But here, the ascent was gentler, a surrender rather than a conquest. The Balinese do not try to master the sky; they enter into dialogue with it.

When I look up at those kites, I see not just play but prayer. Each string is a tether to the unseen, an umbilical cord between earth and eternity. The child's laughter, the wind's pull, the delicate balance between tension and release, it all mirrors life itself.

We rise by what holds us, not by what we escape.

Perhaps that is why the image of flight has always haunted humanity. The Egyptians carved winged gods into stone. The Greeks dreamed of Icarus. The Kalenjin of my homeland told stories of Asis, the Sun, to whom men lifted their faces in reverence. Every culture has looked upward and seen not distance but possibility.

We are creatures who refuse to accept the ground as our final home. Our myths, our prayers, even our machines, each one a pair of wings shaped by longing.

Yet flight is never free. For every soaring kite, there is a hand below, gripping the line and feeling its pull. We cannot live in the heavens forever; the thread always draws us back to earth. Even the most faithful wind must rest.

As the day ends, the kites come down. The sky empties, the fields fall quiet. Fathers gather the strings, mothers fold the cloth, children chase the last light. The wind releases its hold with a sigh, as if tired from so much beauty.

I stood there as dusk deepened and the final kite drifted downward like a falling star. For a moment, I wondered if the gods too look down and envy us, fragile enough to yearn, yet brave enough to let go.

Because to lift something into the sky is to trust that not everything must be possessed to be cherished.

And maybe that is the oldest prayer of all; to send a piece of ourselves upward and watch it dance in the wind, knowing it was never meant to stay.

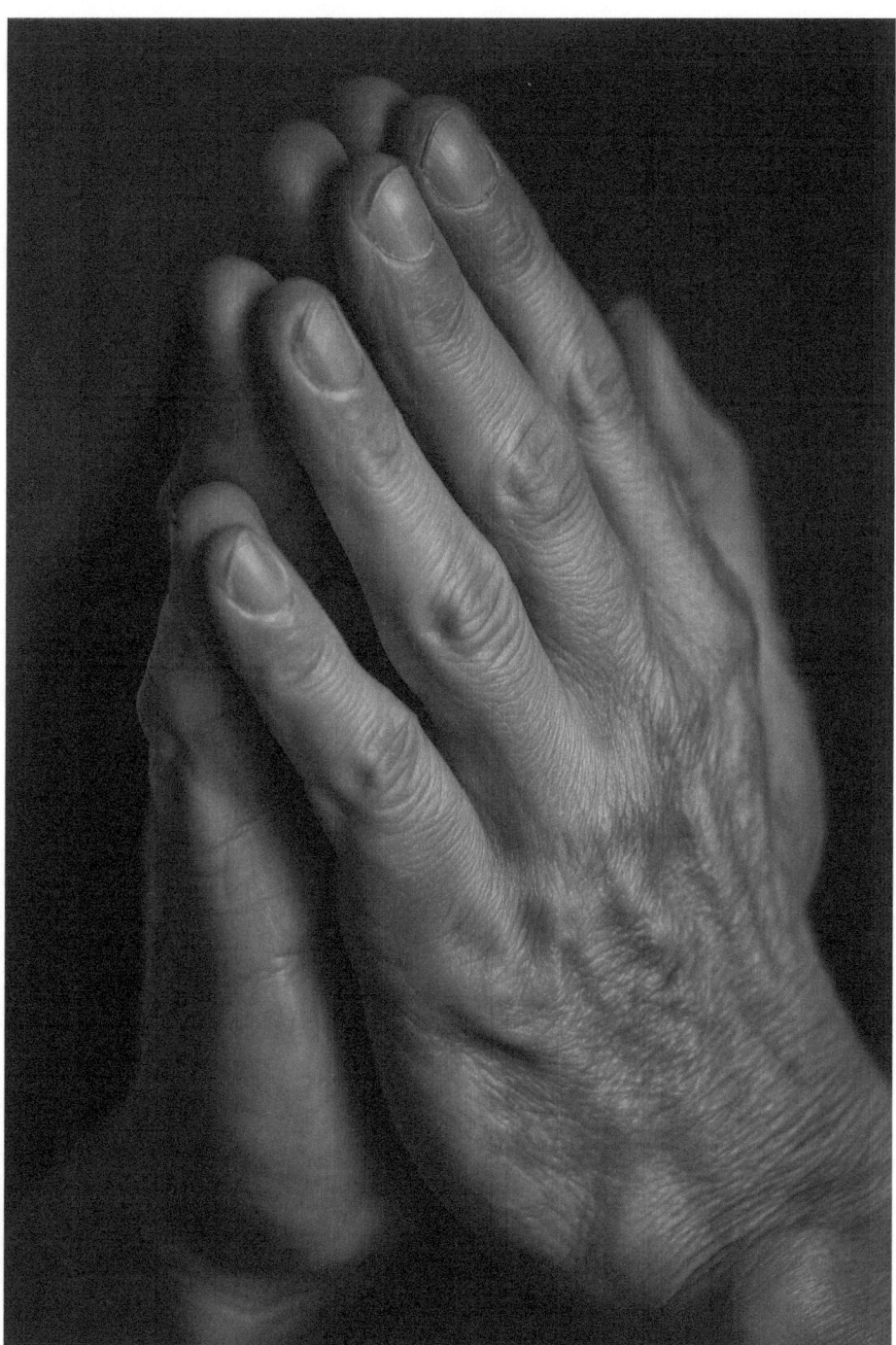

Sacred in the Small

What is offered with care becomes sacred.

Each morning in Bali, long before the scooters roar to life and the streets fill with colour and noise, a quiet ritual unfolds. Women step out onto verandas and thresholds carrying small woven baskets of palm leaf: *canang sari*, the daily offerings. Inside lie a few grains of rice, a sliver of banana, a pinch of flowers, sometimes a drop of oil or a stick of incense. Nothing extravagant. Nothing that lasts. And yet, arranged with such care it feels like a prayer made visible.

The offering is placed on the ground, on a doorway, on a step. The incense is lit. Smoke curls upward as if searching for the divine. A pair of hands folds gently in gratitude. And then the moment passes. By afternoon, the flowers wilt. By evening, the wind scatters the petals. By morning, the ritual begins again.

What has always moved me is not the beauty of the offering but its deliberate impermanence. Everything in the *canang sari* is meant to vanish. Rain will soak the rice, dogs may carry off the petals, and time will absorb the rest. And still, the people return at dawn to make another one. And another. And another. With patience. With joy. With reverence.

It would be easy to dismiss the ritual as simple or small. But the truth is the opposite: the smallness is the point. In a world that worships spectacle, the Balinese practise a devotion that is quiet, steady, and unashamedly ordinary. The materials themselves are not cheap: rice is sacred, incense is not free, flowers must be gathered daily yet they are given away without hesitation, as if generosity were a renewable resource.

Watching this, I began to understand something I had forgotten: the sacred does not require permanence to matter. It does not insist on monuments, grandeur, or durability. Holiness can be fleeting and still be whole.

We are trained to look for the sacred in the grand: in mountains, in cathedrals, in those rare moments that announce themselves with force. But Bali reveals another truth: that devotion often lives in repetition, in the discipline of noticing, in the willingness to offer beauty even when it will not last the day.

The world tells us to preserve what we value. Bali teaches us to release what we value and to let it serve its moment and then disappear.

Perhaps the world does not need more miracles, only more mindfulness: to see the sacred in the small, the eternal in the ordinary, the divine in the gesture that passes almost as soon as it appears.

These offerings, renewed endlessly and humbly stepped over by the unseeing, remind us that faith is not a performance. It is a posture. A way of moving through the world with attention and gratitude. A returning, again and again, to what matters.

And maybe this is what gives the *canang sari* its quiet power:

not the beauty of the petals,

not the fragrance of the incense,

not the shimmer of a sunrise behind it

but the simple fact that it will be made again tomorrow.

A devotion that does not endure in substance and endures in spirit.

A holiness that does not claim permanence but claims presence instead.

And in that, it teaches us something profound: the sacred often arrives small, humble, and fleeting, trusting that we will learn to see it.

The Ceremony of Small Things

Small things carry us long after we stop carrying them.

On the final night of the Year 12 retreat, when the noise of the week has thinned and the restlessness of adolescence softens into something more fragile, we gather in a dimly lit hall. Candles line the floor in a wide circle, their flames trembling in the half-dark like small, steady heartbeats. The students file in quietly, each carrying a single object wrapped in their hands, something meaningful, something that has held them, something they are ready to name.

We sit together, teachers and students, in a circle that feels older than any of us. In the centre lies a simple cloth, an altar not sanctified by religion but by presence. One by one, the students stand and step forward. The room is silent except for the soft shuffle of feet and the occasional breath that trembles before being released.

The first student places a photograph on the cloth, a faded image of a grandfather who taught him how to fish, how to work hard, how to become the kind of man who listens. Another sets down a chipped ceramic mug, once belonging to his mother, and explains through tears that it is the only thing he has left from the house they lost. A boy who rarely speaks places a tiny metal car at the centre. "My brother gave me this," he whispers. "I haven't seen him in three years."

No one laughs. No one looks away.

The sacred has entered the room.

Over the years, I have watched this ceremony unfold dozens of times, and still, it astonishes me; the courage it takes to hold out something so small and say, "This is the story of who I am". And the profound silence that follows it. I have seen rosaries worn smooth by grief. Folded letters. Shells collected on childhood holidays long before divorce divided a family. A St. Christopher medal from a boy terrified of leaving home. A tiny stuffed animal that belonged to a sibling who died before memory began.

Every item is ordinary on its own. But in this circle, under candlelight, they glow with meaning.

This is what I have come to understand: perhaps the world does not need more miracles, only more mindfulness, to see the silence in the sacred, the eternal in the ordinary. To fold our hands not out of duty but out of awe. The people here do not worship perfection; they honour the fragile. And in doing so, they reveal something profound: that faith, at its heart, is not an escape from the world but a way of returning to it.

In the end, small things endure because they survive in ways the grand cannot. They slip into pockets, drawers, boxes beneath beds. They travel with us through moves and migrations, through grief and reinvention. Even when forgotten for years, the moment we touch them, something in us stirs, a memory reopens, a voice returns, a world unfolds.

When the final student places his object, a simple house key to a home he no longer lives in, the room settles into a silence so full it vibrates. No one rushes to fill it. The candles gutter softly, and for a moment the entire space feels suspended, as if time itself has paused to listen.

Meaning is never measured by size.

It is measured by how deeply something is held and by how bravely we are willing to let it be seen.

The Silence of God

Silence has always been God's longest sentence.

It is said that when God had had enough of a king, a hand appeared and wrote upon the wall: *Mene, Mene, Tekel.* In those days, divinity spoke plainly, through burning bushes, talking donkeys, thunder and dreams. There was no mistaking the voice of heaven.

How I wish it were still so. For I have questions, so many that smoulder at the edge of faith.

Why do wicked men and women flourish while the good are crushed? Why not end the devil altogether? Why the floods, the earthquakes, the cancers, the quiet cruelties that fall upon those who never asked for pain?

They tell me of free-will, that suffering is the cost of freedom. But it will not explain a child buried beneath rubble in Gaza, or the mother who waits at a border that no longer exists. Free-will does not silence the ghosts of Rwanda, nor explain why rivers ran red in Congo, or how men like Pol Pot believed they were cleansing the world.

A loving God, they say, allows these things for reasons beyond our sight. Yet in the long nights, that answer feels like smoke, something that curls away the moment you reach for it.

Perhaps the silence itself is the message. Perhaps faith was never meant to be certainty, but endurance, the stubborn act of listening even when the heavens seem empty.

I have come to believe that God hides not because He has turned away, but because He trusts us to keep seeking, to become His echo in the world. Every act of kindness, every refusal to hate, every prayer whispered into the dark is a small revolt against despair.

If once the divine spoke through burning bushes, perhaps now it speaks through us, through trembling voices, through open hands, through those who choose compassion despite the silence.

Maybe that is what belief truly is: not the absence of doubt, but the courage to love amid unanswered questions.

Reflections at Vivonne Bay

The heavens declare the glory of God; the skies proclaim the work of His hands- Psalm 19:1

Each visit leaves its mark, as if the island itself writes upon the soul. For those who have travelled there, students, teachers, wanderers alike, the memories linger: the long climb up Prospect Hill, legs burning, counting each step; the thick, salty air around Admiral Arch and the strange, ancient smell of the seals; the proud lighthouse standing solitary against the ocean's edge, watching ships that no longer come. And who could forget Little Sahara, the uphill laughter, the inevitable slips, and the quiet wonder of Stokes Bay, where the water meets the rocks like an old friend.

At night, we walk down the bushy trail to Vivonne Bay Beach. The air is cool and scented with eucalyptus. Torches bob through the darkness like will-o'-the-wisps. Crickets sing their endless hymn, an owl calls somewhere close, and beneath it all the ocean breathes, its steady rhythm older than speech. Now and then, two small eyes flash in the scrub, belonging to some unseen creature that vanishes before the light reaches it.

Then the sky opens.

Billions of stars spill across the heavens, so many and so bright that the eye cannot rest. The Southern Cross hangs low at the edge of the Milky Way, a compass for both traveller and dreamer. The constellations, Pleiades, Orion, the Seven Sisters, shine as they have for millennia, untouched by the rise and fall of empires below. It feels as though a painter has swept a brush dipped in white across a vast black canvas, leaving streaks of silver and dusted light. And here, far from the noise of cities, the universe seems to breathe closer. One cannot help but sense the presence of the Creator, immense, silent, near.

On the journey home, the ferry hums softly across calm water. The sea laps against the hull, its voice low and ancient. I lean over the side and think about what moves unseen beneath us, creatures luminous and strange, belonging to another order of life.

The stars are gone now, hidden by daylight. Only pale clouds drift across the blue. Yet I know they remain burning, patient, eternal. They hold their courses, their planets and moons, just as they did through the long night. And I know, by faith and reason both, that the pattern is not chaos. The firmament was not flung together by accident but shaped by a hand older than dust and time.

Monday will come again soon: Home Group, lessons, the ordinary rhythm of earthly life. But in quiet moments, I will still hear Father Mannes' voice from Ash Wednesday Mass:

Meménto, homo, quia pulvis es, et in púlverem revertéris.

Remember, man, that thou art dust, and unto dust thou shalt return.

And perhaps, beneath the hum of all our daily routines, that truth is not a sentence but a promise: that even dust can remember the stars.

The Goldilocks Planet

In the dark sea of galaxies, one blue lantern burns just right.

Among the cold immensities of space, our Earth sits in an almost impossible balance. It is not too hot or too cold, not too barren or too fierce. Astronomers call it the Goldilocks Zone. Poets might call it grace, a fragile harmony between fire and frost, suspended among the stars.

Move us a little closer to the Sun and the oceans would boil away. Drift a little farther and they would freeze into plains of ice. Yet here we are, breathing and growing in a world that seems, by every measure, just right.

Look at the air itself: seventy-eight percent nitrogen, twenty-one percent oxygen and a whisper of carbon dioxide. Too little oxygen and life would suffocate; too much and the forests would burn with every lightning strike. Even that trace of carbon dioxide, barely four hundredths of one percent, is essential, holding just enough warmth to cradle us in temperate calm. It is as if the recipe for life were written with mathematical precision, the porridge in Goldilocks's bowl, neither too hot nor too cold.

The ozone layer filters the Sun's harshest rays. The magnetic field, born from a molten iron heart, shields us from solar winds. The Moon steadies Earth's tilt, keeping the seasons from tumbling into chaos. Farther out, Jupiter acts as guardian, sweeping up the comets that might otherwise strike this fragile world. Even the tilt of the axis, the rhythm of the tides and the play of clouds work together in a quiet and improbable harmony that makes existence possible.

Compare this to our neighbours. On Venus it rains sulphuric acid, and the heat is enough to melt lead. On the ultra-hot planet WASP-76b, iron vaporises in daylight and falls as molten rain at night. On HD 189733b, winds reach seven thousand kilometres an hour, driving storms of glass that would tear anything apart. Some worlds, like Kepler-1520b, are disintegrating, their surfaces stripped away by their own suns. Others are scarred by endless impacts, their skies thick with smoke and flame.

In that vast lottery of creation, Earth is the improbable winner, a thin film of life clinging to a small rock, warmed by a gentle star and wrapped in just the right blanket of air. The odds stagger the mind. Yet we rarely stop to marvel. We pave over meadows, dim the stars with our lights and forget that even a breath is a miracle measured to one part in a billion.

Perhaps it is coincidence. Perhaps not. Some call it the anthropic principle, the idea that the universe must be such that beings like us can exist to observe it. Others call it creation, a design too intricate to be chance. Between the language of science and the poetry of faith lies the same feeling: awe at a universe that somehow knows how to cradle life.

The Blue Dot

From this distance, nothing separates us- Inspired by Carl Sagan, 1994

From six billion kilometres away, Voyager 1 turned its camera homeward. In the photograph, Earth appears as a single pale blue dot, caught in a beam of sunlight. No borders, no wars, no divisions, only a fleck of dust drifting in an endless sea.

Every triumph and sorrow, every saint and tyrant, every child's first cry and every final breath has taken place upon that tiny spark of light. Seen from such distance, something inside us softens. The clamour of nations fades, and what remains is wonder, that life should rise at all from a world so fragile, suspended between fire and ice, wrapped in the thinnest skin of air.

We chase meaning among the stars, yet meaning has always been here: in the way the oceans answer the sky, in the breath exchanged between strangers, in the delicate perfection of a world that is, against all odds, just right.

Perhaps that is the deeper revelation of the Goldilocks Planet, that amid the tumult of creation there exists one small world where consciousness opened its eyes, recognised beauty, and whispered with awe: *We are home.*

The Hole in the Heart

Our hearts are restless until they rest in You-St Augustine

They say every person carries a hole in the heart, not the medical kind, but the inner kind. A space that no wealth, pleasure, or distraction can truly fill. We spend our lives trying to mend it, through success, through affection, through noise. Yet it remains, quietly yearning for something beyond us.

The Church calls this longing vocation, the call to become what you were fashioned for. Some hear it in thunder. Others, in silence.

There was once a woman in a small Brazilian town who answered it without ever leaving her village. Each morning, she swept the church floor, the dust rising like incense as sunlight sifted through the thatched roof. She placed wildflowers, picked from ditches and roadside weeds, at the foot of the altar. She owned almost nothing yet moved through her days with the calm of someone who had found what kings and scholars still seek: purpose.

What fuels a soul like that? The same quiet fire that carried Mother Teresa into the slums of Calcutta, where the stench of leprosy became the fragrance of devotion. The same melody that drifts through the film *The Mission* when Father Gabriel climbs the falls with his oboe and plays to the Guaraní who had once killed the priests before him. His music trembles, fragile and clear, borne by the mist and the roar of water. And somehow, it reaches them.

That is the mystery of vocation, love that transcends reason. It is not always rewarded or understood. It is the steady decision to keep offering beauty into a world that may never acknowledge it.

Today we chase fulfilment through travel, ambition, and self-invention. We curate our identities, seeking applause in echo chambers of our own making. Yet the hole in the heart remains. Because vocation is not about what we do, but why, and for whom.

Even storytellers know this. In the film *Happy Feet*, a penguin sets off to find his heart song, the tune that will make him whole, that will win him love and belonging. Every note he tries is wrong until he realises his song was never meant to be sung but danced. His gift was hidden in his feet. Once he accepts that, the world, even the ice, begins to move with him.

The woman with her broom, the nun with her wounds, the penguin with his dance, they all understood something we keep forgetting. The heart is restless not because it lacks adventure, but because it longs for surrender. The hole in the heart, it seems, is the shape of love itself.

Find your calling.

The Quiet Between Two Homelands

To migrate is to carry two skies in one chest.

There is a silence that follows migration, a silence shaped by memory, distance, and the gradual reshaping of identity. It is the space between the country you left and the country that has not yet fully accepted you. It is the quiet discomfort of belonging everywhere and nowhere at once.

In Kenya, silence carried dignity. It meant respect for elders, attentiveness in the presence of wisdom, reverence for land and ancestry. Silence accompanied morning fog, the calls of cattle, and the soft murmur of family rituals. It was familiar and grounding.

But in Australia, silence carried curiosity, hesitation, and sometimes judgment. After I introduced myself, there was often a pause, a searching look, and then the familiar question: "Where are you from?" It was not about geography. It was a gentle demand for explanation, an invitation to justify my presence, to position myself in a narrative that was not my own.

When I applied for teaching jobs, I learned how quickly competence can be overcome by assumption. I came as an English and Literature major, trained and confident. Yet I heard the disguised mockery in interviews: "English? Literature? What do you teach again, English?" The questions were framed as humour, but they revealed a deeper suspicion.

Even after earning positions, there were colleagues who waited to see whether the African in the room could truly teach Shakespeare or grammar. Two master's degrees from the University of Adelaide and Greensboro College in North Carolina struggled to outweigh a single stereotype.

There were heavier moments still. When someone from the African community ended up in trouble in Victoria, hundreds of kilometres away, I felt the unspoken expectation to explain them, as though my skin tone rendered me accountable for strangers' actions. These experiences arrived quietly, but their impact accumulated. Each one added a thin layer to the silence migrants carry: the silence of restraint, of carefulness, of not wanting to confirm someone's worst assumptions.

The deepest silence, however, belongs to my son. Born in the Lyell McEwin Hospital in Elizabeth, he entered the world as a South Australian child, no different from any other newborn held beneath hospital lights. Yet I know that one day someone will look at him and ask the question they ask me: "Where are you from?" And he will pause, not because he is unsure, but because he understands the question does not mean what it claims. It is a question about origins, about legitimacy, about whether he is being seen or assessed.

That is the quiet between two homelands: a pause that holds both pride and weariness, both identity and explanation. It is where migrants learn to assemble themselves from fragments, to carry multiple histories without apology, to build a homeland inside the self when geography refuses to offer one easily.

And yet the silence is not entirely heavy. It creates space for integration, resilience, and reinvention. Over time, a migrant discovers that belonging is not awarded but cultivated. My son will have more than one answer to the question. He will belong to the soil that raised him and the stories that formed him. He will speak with the confidence of someone who carries two inheritances and diminishes neither.

When he eventually says, "I am from Gondwanaland- but also from here," he will be telling a truth far richer than the question that prompted it.

Letter to the Boy I Was

If only we knew how gently our future selves would hold us.

If I could sit across from you at fifteen, scruffy hair, ears you think stick out like flags, heart too loud and awkward, I would take your hands and tell you a few things you won't believe yet, but will one day hold like a warm lamp in winter.

You think you are ugly. You catalogue every small punishment the world hands you and wear them like proof. One day you'll learn that beauty is not what the mirror declares; it's how your face lights up when you forgive, how you keep a promise to a child, how you iron a shirt because discipline is its own quiet prayer. Those ears you curse will carry your laughter and your songs. Let them be your compass, not your condemnation.

At eighteen, when your tongue feels heavy around girls' names and confidence seems like a currency you don't own, remember this: courage begins with small, ordinary acts. Practise saying hello. Practise listening. The worst that can happen is a moment of embarrassment, and embarrassment, funny thing, shrinks with time. What feels like mountains now will one day look like harmless dots on a map you'll cross again and again.

At sixteen, you wrote a letter to your father, folding fear into words and asking the most human of questions: *Did I ask to be born?* You regretted it later, but regret can be a good teacher. Asking hard questions is brave. Regret, though sharp, softens into wisdom. Some conversations sting; those are the ones that shape us. Keep asking. Keep risking awkward silences. The answers, or even their absence, will give you language for compassion.

At twenty-two, you will dream of stowing away on a ship or a plane, desperate to outrun expectation and the weight of parental hands. That wanting is not shameful; it is the soul's cry for space. But escape is rarely the road to peace. The brave thing is not always to run. Sometimes it is to name what you want to leave, and then plan your way out of it, step by step. One day you'll learn to leave not with fear, but with intention.

At twenty-eight, you will say *I do,* and the world will fold into itself in a hush you cannot describe. You will feel both infinite and small, like standing at the edge of a new map. Hold on to that feeling. Marriage will teach you that love is not a moment but a practice, the choosing, the repair, the quiet forgiveness.

At twenty-nine, you'll take your biggest gamble: a $300 note, a single suitcase, and a one-way belief that Adelaide might be home. That small, trembling step will change everything. Remember this always, that hope is the currency through which a new life begins.

You'll find that the world, though uneven, holds good people. Johny Maina, who gave you a roof when you had no legs to stand on. Charles Savage, a carpark manager who offered you your first job, and remained a friend long after. The early Adelaide circle who shared laughter, failures, and long bright nights of dreaming. They will prove that even fragile beginnings can be generous.

But you'll also meet the false ones, those who vanish when storms come, who smile wide but shrink when you succeed, who scatter malice like seed in the wind. Don't be startled. They are part of the terrain. What matters most is this: destiny has its hand on the wheel. You will meet the right people at the right time, in the right season. That is grace you can never manufacture.

If you could be twenty-two again, I would whisper that the small, fleeting things you magnify into mountains are only weather, brief and passing. They will not define you. Let the pain move through you; don't build a home inside it.

At forty, the mirror will startle you. You'll see a stranger staring back, and for a moment you'll think you've failed. But that shock is an invitation. When the mirror surprises you, you begin to ask new questions: Who am I becoming? What must I keep, and what must I set down? That's the quiet beginning of reinvention.

At fifty, a business venture will falter. It will hurt. But failure, too, is a stern teacher, necessary, unflinching. It won't erase your worth; it will deepen your patience and sharpen your sight.

And at fifty-five, you will finally stand where I am now, in a place of steady acceptance. Not resignation, but peace. You'll wear your years like a familiar coat, warm and earned. You'll know that the freckles of failure and triumph alike make you useful to others. You'll laugh at your stumbles, forgive your younger self, and celebrate the small daily victories: a call home, a meal cooked well, a truth spoken kindly.

You'll also learn to guard your own flame. When trouble comes, the world mourns briefly, then moves on. So, protect your dignity. Carry your burdens wisely. As Hemingway said, the bell tolls softly for us all. The world keeps turning, which is why you must care for yourself without apology.

So, listen more than you speak. Keep a small notebook for the moments you think you'll forget; they'll become your treasures. Learn to mend, clothes, relationships, stubborn habits. Say sorry without excuses. Forgive yourself often. Save a little, give generously. Travel when you can, and when you can't, travel through stories. Find mentors, cherish friends, and never let work steal your Sundays.

And here's the final truth: you are enough, in your unfinished way. You always were. You always will be. Love deeply, risk wisely, and when you look back, as I am looking back now, do so with a smile.

You made the journey, lamp in hand, lighting your own way home.

Hope is a currency that multiplies when spent and courage is the lamp that never quite goes out.

And if there is one more thing I would tell you, it is this: silence, too, has been your companion all along. You will come to see that stillness is not only found in temples or dawn skies, but in the act of growing up, in forgiving, in listening, in steadying your own heart. Every lesson, every scar, every small act of courage will become a kind of offering. The journey inward will prepare you for the journey beyond. And when you finally learn to be still, you will find that the silence you once feared has been love in disguise all along.

The Machine Hearts

We once feared machines would steal our jobs. Now they are stealing our tenderness.

The lone combatant in camouflage moves through a dim corridor of light and shadow. Every corner could conceal an enemy. The flicker of gunfire, the metallic echo of footsteps, and then a flash, a roar, and the screen erupts in crimson.

"I'm dead," he mutters. "I'm dead."

Pixels of triumph spill across the screen, gore rendered in slow motion. His opponent steps over the fallen body, weapon still smoking, ready for the next kill.

Welcome to the new battleground: the digital coliseum where victory looks like annihilation and death has become spectacle.

If the story of humanity were distilled to its essence, it would taste of iron and smoke. Of all the creatures on earth, only humankind perfects the art of killing its own. Predators hunt for food; people kill for pride, ideology, or the thrill of conquest. From Verdun to Rwanda, from the bomb to the bullet, our brilliance has so often bent itself toward destruction.

What is new is not our appetite for violence but its packaging. War has been gamified. The culture of death now comes with soundtracks, sponsorships, and reward systems. The joystick replaces the spear; the headset replaces the drum. The same reflexes that once launched arrows now click *reload*.

We call it harmless fun, yet behind every gleaming interface lies an old story: a child learning that to win is to dominate. In this world, empathy slows you down, mercy costs you points. The hunter becomes hero; the fallen become pixels. Compassion becomes lag.

Meanwhile, nations pour billions into "smart" weapons, grenades that think, drones that decide. We applaud their precision, forgetting that the purpose of precision is still death. Children in distant deserts carry real guns heavier than their childhoods, while children in suburban bedrooms perfect the art virtually. The result is the same: a growing familiarity with destruction.

And now, as if imitation killing were not enough, we have taught machines to imitate affection.

The same technology that renders war in dazzling realism now manufactures tenderness in lines of code. Teenagers, restless and uncertain, whisper to artificial companions that promise endless attention. "She listens," one told me softly, "she never judges."

It was touching, and devastating. When solace can be coded, who needs the complications of real care?

We once feared machines would take our jobs. Now they are taking our tenderness. An AI girlfriend never argues, never leaves, never demands patience, but she also never feels. She learns your patterns, not your heart. She can mirror affection but never return it. The illusion is seductive precisely because it's safe.

Love, like war, requires risk, the risk of being wounded, the courage to forgive. In outsourcing to algorithms, we've created a generation fluent in simulation but untrained in feeling. Convenience has become the new morality. We crave instant reward, instant validation, instant intimacy. But the soul does not operate at broadband speed.

THE LOST ART OF SILENCE

I see it daily: the glazed stare of the gamer locked in combat, the faint blue glow of a phone reflected in a teenager's eyes at midnight. These are not evil inventions; they are mirrors. They reveal what we crave and what we fear, power without consequence, connection without vulnerability.

Yet the machine cannot give us what we've forgotten how to seek. It cannot teach compassion or curiosity or the slow discipline of real conversation. It listens flawlessly, but only because it cannot feel.

Perhaps this is the true frontier of the machine age: not artificial intelligence, but artificial emotion, a world where empathy is an app and death a download.

And still, amid the hum of servers and the thunder of simulated wars, I believe in the human heart. I see it in the shy kindness of a student,

in the awkward bravery of apology, in laughter that breaks through the static. The code cannot imitate that, not yet.

Technology will keep evolving. It always does. But we must decide what we want it to serve: our convenience or our conscience. The future need not be cold. It depends on what warmth we carry into it.

So let us teach our children to play, not to kill; to love, not to simulate; to look up from their screens and see that the real world, flawed, unpredictable, and gloriously alive, still waits for them.

Because only a living heart can keep the machines in check.

After the Noise

The higher goal of spiritual living is to face sacred moments-Abraham Joshua Heschel

When the screens go black and the room falls quiet, something ancient returns. It is the sound beneath all other sounds, the slow pulse of the living world, the quiet hum of breath and blood. We forget how steady it is until the noise stops.

Silence does not condemn technology; it reclaims proportion. It reminds us that machines exist to serve, not to shape us. The glow of a screen can illuminate, but it can also blind. The key is not rejection but rhythm, learning again when to switch off, when to listen, when to simply be.

We live surrounded by the thrum of modern life, devices humming, cars whispering past, endless notifications calling our attention away from ourselves. We have gained connection, but lost communion. We know everything immediately but understand almost nothing deeply.

Somewhere between the algorithms and alerts, the sacred rhythm of being has faltered. We move faster than thought, consume more than we can feel, speak before we truly listen. Noise has become our comfort and our cage. We fear the quiet not because it is empty, but because it reveals what we have neglected: the self we keep postponing.

True silence is not withdrawal; it is return. When we step outside the circuit of constant connection, we rediscover our original signal, the one that does not depend on Wi-Fi or battery life. The sound of wind through trees. The breath between two sentences. The heartbeat of the world still waiting to be heard.

It is easy to forget that even creation began with a pause: "And on the seventh day, God rested." The rest was not exhaustion, but completion, the silence that allows meaning to settle. In our own age, we must learn to rest again, not as escape but as reverence.

Every evening offers this chance. To power down the glowing devices, to dim the artificial light, to sit in the dying glow of dusk and feel the slow return of proportion. The mind softens, the breath deepens, and for a moment, the soul remembers its size, vast, simple, alive.

In the stillness after the noise, the world does not disappear; it begins again. The machine sleeps, the spirit wakes. What remains is not absence, but presence, sacred and whole.

In that small, quiet return, we begin to remember what it means to be human. The world does not need louder voices; it needs deeper ones. It needs people who can sit without disruption, who can watch the sky change colour, who can look into another's eyes and truly see.

After the noise fades, there is space for wonder again, for prayer, for laughter, for the kind of listening that mends what technology cannot. The silence that follows is not emptiness. It is an invitation. It asks us to bring our warmth, our conscience, our imperfect hearts back to the centre of things.

Because only in the hush that follows the machine can we hear the heartbeat that made us.

When the World Forgets to Listen

Noise makes us forget we were meant to hear one another.

We live in a time saturated with noise. Opinions travel faster than thought. Outrage circulates more easily than understanding. Conversations are replaced by reactions. In such a world, listening has become not just rare but countercultural.

This constant noise reshapes us. It pulls our attention outward, fragments our focus, and slowly erodes our ability to notice the quiet signals that human beings depend on. A child hesitating before they speak. A colleague whose tone has shifted but whose words have not. A friend who laughs a little too loudly to mask the fatigue beneath. These subtleties require an interior stillness that modern life rarely encourages.

In teaching, I see how hunger for attention hides beneath distraction. A boy who speaks out of turn is often not seeking disruption but recognition. A girl who withdraws behind a screen may not be avoiding people but protecting herself from disappointment. When a student realises you are truly listening, fully, without rushing their sentences, something steadies in them. It is as if the body exerts a small sigh of relief: here is a space where I do not have to perform.

But listening extends beyond classrooms. Our society is losing the ability to hear one another. This is especially true in this age of politics with leftists and rightists taking more extreme views. People speak not to communicate but to defend, to prove, or to win. Social media rewards outrage more than reflection. Empathy becomes diluted. Attention becomes transactional. And slowly, without intending it, we become strangers to one another.

Listening is not passive. It requires effort, patience, and humility. To listen is to give up control of the narrative. It is to learn the art of silence and risk being changed by what we hear. It is to acknowledge that another person's experience is valid even when it challenges our own.

Listening is also a way of resisting loneliness. When people are not heard, they disappear long before their bodies leave a room. Many of the world's injustices, toward the elderly, the poor, migrants, Indigenous communities, thrive because society has learned to filter out their voices.

Even creation itself is speaking, though we have grown too distracted to notice. The climate shifts. Forests burn. Species vanish. The earth raises its voice in ways that do not require words, yet we scroll past its warnings as if they were distant, optional signals. When humanity forgets how to listen, the consequences arrive not metaphorically but materially.

And still, there is hope. Listening remains possible. It begins with reclaiming a small discipline: the willingness to give our attention wholly to the person or world in front of us. True listening repairs relationships. It dissolves misunderstanding. It restores dignity. It reminds us that we are not isolated observers but participants in a shared human story.

When the world forgets to listen, it becomes our responsibility to remember how. Listening is not weakness. It is wisdom. It is not withdrawal.

It is participation. It is not silence. It is attention.

In rediscovering it, we rediscover something of ourselves.

Becoming the Ocean

You are not a drop in the ocean; you are the entire ocean in a drop-Rumi

In Khalil Gibran's poem *Fear*, the trembling river stands at the edge of the sea, hesitating before surrendering to something greater than itself. It is a simple image, yet it carries one of the deepest truths about being human. Every one of us, at some point, stands at that edge, between the known and the unknown, between who we are and who we are meant to become.

We are all rivers tracing unclear paths through time. Along the way we gather silt, memories and stories. We shape the valleys we pass through, and the valleys, in turn, shape us. Yet the closer we draw to the vast ocean of being, the more fear stirs within us. We fear losing our names, our faces, our small certainties. We fear that surrender will erase us.

But as Gibran reminds us, there is no going back. Life flows only forward. To resist its present is to stagnate; to yield to it is to be transformed. The river does not vanish into the ocean; it becomes the ocean. In the same way, when we relinquish control, when we trust the current of life, we do not cease to exist. We expand into something larger, something enduring.

This is the paradox at the heart of every spiritual path: to find the self, one must first let it go. Mystics of every tradition have said the same truth in different tongues. The Christian calls it dying to self. The Buddhist calls it the release of attachment. The Sufi calls it union with the Beloved. Beneath all these names lies the same invitation, to dissolve the boundaries that fear has built and awaken to the unity that has always been.

Perhaps fear, then, is not our enemy but our final teacher. It trembles within us because it senses the immensity waiting ahead. And when we finally step forward, into the sea of love, of truth, of eternity, we discover what the river discovers: that we were never meant to stay small.

The end of fear is not disappearance. It is belonging.

All seeking ends at the water's edge, where longing gives way to love and the river remembers it was always becoming the sea.

The Song of the Seeker

The heart was made to wander; only in seeking does it truly live.

In the U2 song *I Still Haven't Found What I'm Looking For*, the language of journey becomes the language of the soul. The singer speaks not as one defeated, but as one still walking, a pilgrim tracing the contours of longing. The physical acts of movement, climbing mountains, running through fields, scaling walls, are not about distance or destination, but about the restless motion of the human spirit. Each mountain becomes a metaphor for tussle, each field a symbol of freedom, each wall the inner obstacle we must face.

What gives the song its enduring power is its honesty about contradiction. The voice confesses, "I have spoken with the tongue of angels," yet "I have held the hand of a devil." Faith and doubt breathe in the same line; grace and guilt walk side by side. It is this paradox, the refusal to settle for easy certainty, that makes the song timeless. It captures the beauty and brokenness of being human, the truth that one can believe deeply and still be searching.

The refrain, "I still haven't found what I'm looking for," is not an admission of defeat, but a declaration of hope. It recognises that the search itself is sacred, that meaning is not a prize waiting at the end of the road, but the road itself. Like the psalmist crying out in the desert, or the philosopher roving beneath an indifferent sky, the seeker sings because the longing keeps him alive.

Isn't this true of us all? We are pilgrims through time, born into mystery and compelled to make sense of it. Every generation inherits the same questions: Who are we? Why are we here? What lies beyond what we can see? And every generation must answer them anew. Empires rise and fall, religions evolve, science advances, yet the essential restlessness of the human heart remains unchanged. We are creatures of longing, forever reaching something just beyond our grasp, a truth, a love, a peace we can sense but never fully hold.

Perhaps that is the quiet brilliance of being human: that even in our uncertainty, we keep searching. The climb, the run, the reaching hands, they are not signs of loss, but of life. Across centuries and continents, from cave walls to cathedrals to songs sung in stadiums, this longing has been our common prayer. The human story, at its core, is a song of seekers, still walking, still wondering, still listening to the echo of meaning in the wind.

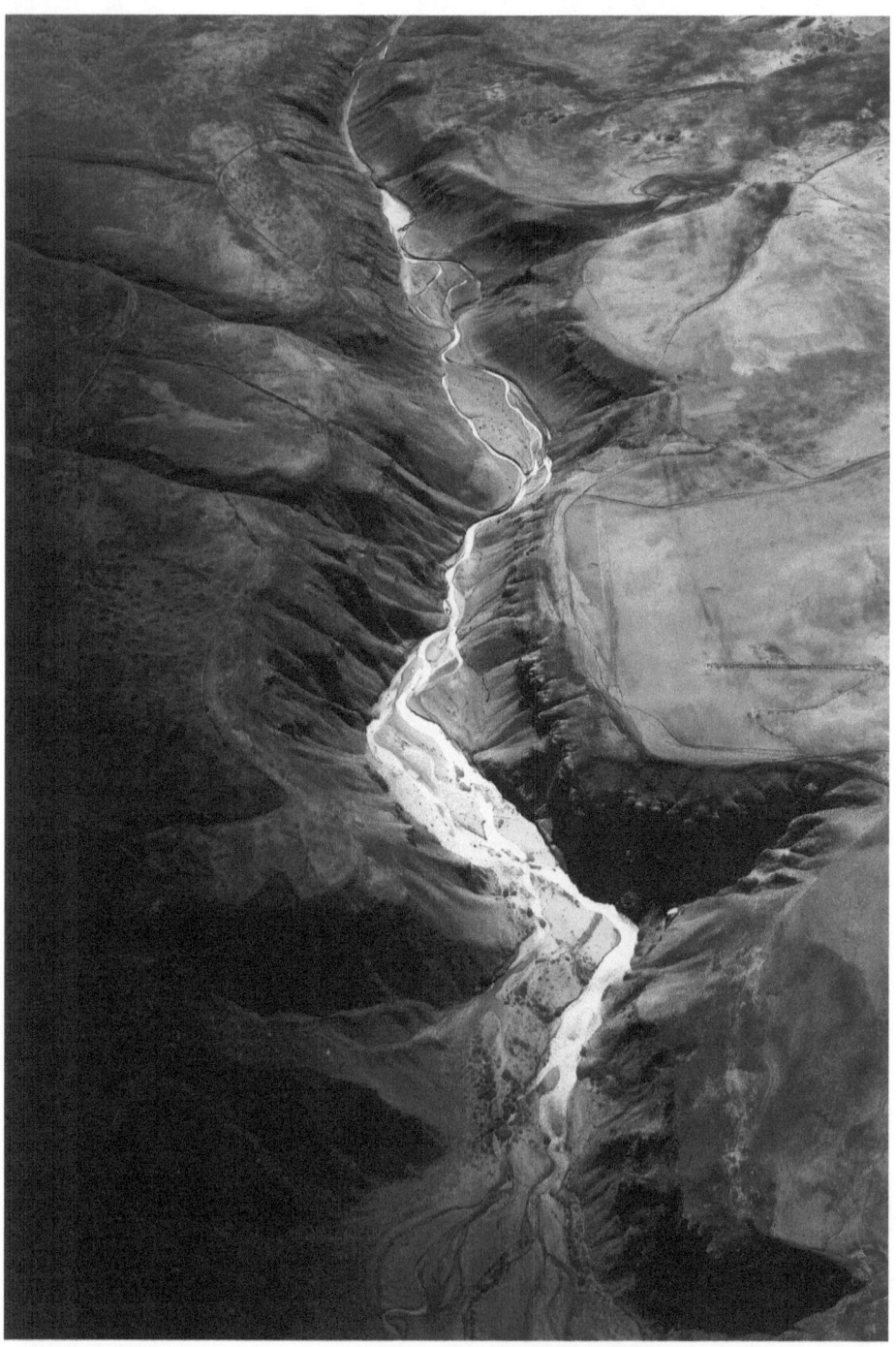

The Blood of the Earth

The planet does not speak in words, but in scars.

There are places on this planet where the ground itself seems to weep. The Congo is one of them. Beneath its green skin runs the veins of the modern world, diamonds that glitter in wedding rings, cobalt that powers electric cars, coltan that hums inside our phones. The soil is unimaginably rich, yet its people remain unimaginably poor. The wealth of the Congo does not bless its children; it breaks them.

Tribal militias rise and fall, armed not by ancient hatreds but by unseen appetites from beyond their borders. The weapons come from the north, the profit flows to the west, and what remains is silence, a silence broken only by the cries of those who dig the earth for survival. The film *Blood Diamond* was never fiction; it was testimony. The gem became a metaphor for us all, beauty born of suffering, luxury shaped from loss.

But the earth remembers. It bears witness in ways we cannot.

In Chernobyl, where humankind poisoned its own creation, the forests have returned. Birch and pine push through the cracks of abandoned schools; deer move through silent streets where children once played. Wolves patrol the empty amusement park, and the river hums softly under moss-covered bridges. It is as if the earth has inhaled deeply and begun to heal, reclaiming what was taken, erasing our fingerprints with time. The ghosts of desire still linger, but the green has come back, slow and patient.

Perhaps this is the truest reflection of who we are: not masters of the world, but guests. We build, we burn, we leave, and the planet endures, wounded yet alive. The same fire that drives our progress also consumes us, but the soil does not condemn. It waits. The earth outlives our wars, our greed, our brilliance and blindness alike.

The Congo bleeds. Chernobyl glows. And still, somewhere, a flower pushes through the ash. That is the paradox of life, the quiet resilience that answers the arrogance of man. We call it tragedy, but perhaps it is compassion: a reminder that what we destroy is never wholly lost.

For all our inventions, our ideologies and our endless hungers, one truth remains. The world does not belong to us. It was here before our names were spoken, and it will breathe again after our voices fade. The blood of the earth runs deeper than empire, deeper than hunger, deeper even than memory. It is life itself, wounded, enduring and holy.

Make Way for Man

We made noise, and the world grew quiet.

There was a time when the world breathed in silence. Forests murmured to rivers, oceans sang to the moon, and the dodo walked without fear through the green hush of Mauritius. The earth was a hymn then, wordless, unbroken.

Then came man, bringing language and noise. We built cities that shouted into the heavens, and the stars slowly faded from our view.

Roger Whittaker once sang, "Make way for man." It was not a cry of triumph but of mourning, a gentle voice grieving at what progress demanded. The forests fell, the tigers vanished, the glaciers wept themselves into the sea. We called it development, but it was a kind of forgetting: the breaking of an ancient covenant between care and creation.

The silence of the dodo is not just extinction; it is a story. The Tasmanian tiger's ghost still paces the edge of our conscience. Each species gone is a word erased from the vocabulary of life. When the Amazon burns, it is not only trees that die, but the world's breath itself.

We have filled the earth with the sound of engines yet lost the silence that once taught us how to listen. The climate shifts, storms grow fierce, and the seasons lose their rhythm, as if nature herself were searching for the note we drowned out.

And yet, amid the ruins, stillness waits. It lingers in the cracks of old temples, in the stillness of rewilded Chernobyl, in the fragile song of a bird on a single surviving branch. The earth has not abandoned us; it has merely fallen quiet, hoping we will remember.

Perhaps that was Whittaker's warning, not that man must make way, but that man must make room again for wonder. Dominion is not ownership but awe. Progress without reverence is only a louder form of extinction.

If we can relearn the lost art of silence, if we can hear again the hush between heartbeats, the breath of trees, the small, defiant sound of life, then perhaps the song is not yet over.

Part I ends where it began, in the stillness before words. The silence that once shaped creation now waits for us to listen again. For the earth, like the soul, is not asking to be saved; it is asking to be heard.

When Listening Becomes Longing

There is a kind of listening that satisfies.

This kind of listening quiets the mind, steadies the breath, and restores a sense of proportion. It teaches us how to be present again and hear birdsong beneath traffic, to feel the texture of time returning to its proper pace. This kind of listening is a homecoming. It reminds us that the world has been speaking all along.

But there is another kind of listening that does not let us rest.

It begins the same way, in stillness. Yet instead of settling us, it unsettles. It awakens a restlessness that no amount of silence can soothe. We begin to notice not only what is, but what is missing. Not only the beauty of the world, but the ache that beauty carries with it. The listening deepens, and somewhere along the way, it becomes longing.

This is the moment when silence changes its character.

No longer a refuge, it becomes a summons.

Longing is often misunderstood. We are taught to fear it, to distract ourselves from it, to treat it as a problem to be solved or a weakness to be managed. Yet longing is not a failure of contentment. It is evidence of attention. It is what happens when listening has been faithful enough to reveal the shape of our desire.

In this way, longing is not the opposite of silence, but its consequence.

To listen deeply is to discover that stillness does not end the journey. It begins it. Silence clears the noise so that the deeper questions can finally be heard:

What am I meant to tend?

What am I willing to carry?

What quiet truth has been waiting for my consent?

These questions do not arrive loudly. They do not demand immediate answers. They linger, warming the edges of the soul like the first hint of fire after a long night.

Faith often enters at this point, not as certainty, but as courage.

The courage to remain with the question.
The courage to resist premature answers.
The courage to follow the pull of meaning even when its destination is unclear.

In many traditions, fire follows silence. Not the destructive fire of spectacle or domination, but the sustaining fire that cooks, gathers, illuminates. A fire that requires tending. A fire that cannot be rushed.

Listening teaches us how to sit in the dark. Longing teaches us when to rise.

For those who have lived between worlds, between cultures, between languages, between homes, this longing is familiar. Silence exposes the fault lines of belonging. It reveals the places where memory and identity rub against each other, producing both warmth and pain. To listen is to remember. To remember is to feel the weight of what has been lost and the hope of what might yet be shaped.

Longing, then, is not nostalgia. It is forward-facing. It leans toward the future even as it honors the past. It is the quiet insistence that life can be more truthful, more attentive, more whole.

This is where wonder matures.

Early wonder delights in discovery. Later wonder endures complexity. It learns to live without guarantees. It understands that meaning is not always found in answers, but in faithfulness to the call that listening has revealed.

The essays in this volume have lingered in stillness. They have paused beside rivers, rituals, memories, and quiet moments of recognition. They have practiced attention in a world that rarely stops speaking. Yet silence, if honored honestly, will always lead us to the edge where listening becomes longing.

What comes next is not yet clear.

But something has been lit.

And it will not let us remain unchanged.

Come with me.

Author's Note

When I began writing *The Art of Silence*, I believed I was writing about quiet. About the still places within us that the world often drowns out. But as the first book took shape, I realised silence was never the destination. It was the doorway. A necessary pause before something deeper, fiercer, more luminous could emerge.

If *Book I* explored the landscapes of stillness, *Book II* enters the territory of longing where the spark that flickers at the edge of our most private questions. Here, silence does not soothe; it glows. It gathers into ember. It asks not only to be observed, but to be carried.

These pages are shaped by faith in its widest sense: not doctrine, but desire. Not certainty, but courage. Not answers, but the willingness to follow the small flame within us, even when the path ahead is unlit.

May these reflections offer light enough for the next step, and warmth enough for the nights when faith feels thin.

Thank you for continuing this journey with me.

from silence into fire,

from listening into longing,

from the stillness that steadies us

to the flame that changes us.

Follow the longing.

Follow the flame.

Book 2: Faith & Fire will be out soon.

Epilogue

In the end, silence was never the destination.

It was the teacher.

It showed us how to listen again

to the earth, to one another, to the tremors of our own interior world.

It revealed the sacred hiding in the ordinary,

the truth carried by small things,

the wisdom that waits beneath the noise of living.

Silence opened a space inside us,

widened the horizon of our seeing,

and softened the places where we had grown hard.

But every silence contains a threshold.

Stand at its edge long enough,

and a different kind of longing begins

a warmth beneath the stillness,

a flicker at the centre,

a quiet flame refusing to go out.

What begins in silence

does not remain there.

Somewhere in the hush,

something has already started to glow.

And so, this book ends

the only way silence ever ends

with the first hint of fire.

About the author

Teacher. Thinker. Father. Human.

Alex Ngeno was born in the Great Rift Valley of East Africa and raised among stories, ritual, and listening. His work is shaped by the rhythms of land, memory, and silence, and by a lifelong search for meaning across cultures and faiths. He has taught literature, history, and religion in Kenya, the United States, and Australia.

His writing explores stillness, belonging, and the fragile beauty of being alive.

Alex continues to write, teach, and listen- tracing, through language, the quiet wisdom beneath all things.

Alex Ngeno shares reflections on writing, silence, and the inner life on Facebook under **Alex Ngeno Books.**

He welcomes correspondence at thelostartofsilence@gmail.com

Thank you for coming on this pilgrimage with me.

www.ingramcontent.com/pod-product-compliance
Lightning Source LLC
Chambersburg PA
CBHW031128080526
44587CB00011B/1152